MW01469899

VOLUME 1

100 STEPS
With God

Inspiring messages that will strengthen your faith

SPECIAL EDITION

STEVE MCDONALD

Copyright © 2023 by Steve McDonald

All rights reserved.

No portion of this book may be reproduced in any form without written permission from the publisher or author, except as permitted by U.S. copyright law.

Book Cover by Michelle Sojin Cho

Scripture taken from the New King James Version®. Copyright © 1982 by Thomas Nelson. Used by permission. All rights reserved.

Dedicated to my grandmother,

Maizie Lee James

Contents

Acknowledgments xii

About this Book xvi

How to Be a Light to the World 21
   Help Those Who Are in Need

How to Be a Light to the World 29
   Do No Harm

How to Be a Light to the World 37
   Honor Your Temple

How to Be a Light to the World 45
   Pray

How to Be a Light to the World 53
   Acts of Kindness

God in the Workplace 61
   Ways to Walk With God at Work

God In The Workplace 69
   Ways to Walk With God With Coworkers

Don't Get Bitter 84

Will He Say Yes, or No? 92

Celebrate in Your Trials 100

God Is Preparing You and Your Path 108

When It Seems All Is Lost 116

Who Do You Follow? 124

Keep Yourself Unspotted From the World 132

God Has Not Forgotten You 140

Breaking Away From Bondage 148

In the Face of Uncertainty 156

Clay for the Potter 166

When God Wants Your Attention 173

Fighting Doubt 180

Why Should You Love Your Enemies? 188

Divine Perfection in Imperfection 196

Unanswered Prayer 205
    Is It God or You?

Trust in God's Plan, Not Your Own 213

Vengeance Is Mine 221

Waiting on God 229
    Waiting Out of Fear

Waiting on God 237
    Waiting on a Need

Waiting on God 245
    Making a Decision

Freedom in Surrender 253
    5 Ways You Can Experience Captivity When You Turn From God

Freedom in Surrender 261
    5 Ways You Can Experience Freedom When You Turn to God

How to Give Your Heart Fully to God 269

God Is in the Room 277

Closing Prayer 285

Notes 287

Acknowledgments

100 Steps With God was an idea I explored as I contemplated ways to expand the reach and impact of messages for an online ministry I founded in 2022, Walking in Step With God Ministries.

One of the ways our ministry provides a preview of each week's message is to share *quotes* from the upcoming message. Over time, I have witnessed the extent to which our online community has truly enjoyed and engaged with these quotes. It occurred to me that if the community finds such enjoyment and inspiration in these quotes, then others outside of the community may find enjoyment and inspiration as well. This book, the first in a series, is a collection of quotes from messages over the time period of August 2022 to August 2023. We plan to release a new volume for the series each year with 100 new quotes of encouragement from messages.

First and foremost, I need to thank God for this amazing privilege to be used as a vessel to share wisdom. I do not take credit for the contents of this book, or the messages I record nearly every week. I credit the Holy Spirit. You see, before each message, I ask the Holy Spirit what I should say about a particular topic. Two to three hours later I have words of wisdom that I would have never thought to say on my own. I imagine this is what is meant by 'God breathed'.

I have truly enjoyed and continue to enjoy the process of learning and forming a style of transparency and straightforwardness in Walking in Step With God messages. I think it is very important to keep it real as much as possible as we examine the intersection of our day-to-day lives and our walk with God.

I feel blessed to be used as a vessel to share encouragement about a relationship with God and I know I have so much more to learn and opportunities to grow.

The list of people to thank for this book is long, but in this first volume I would like to acknowledge the people who have been involved in supporting the ministry from day one and its continued growth.

I'd like to thank my dear friends Anastasia and Shwarnim for providing me a safe space to share my walk with God with you. Each of you has played a vital role in helping me to understand the opportunity to share my experiences with the world. Without the two of you, this ministry would not have started and this book would not exist.

I would also like to thank the people who have been fans and supporters of Walking in Step With God Ministries from day 1. Many thanks to Jennifer, Enoch,

Acknowledgments

Derrick, Philip, Kris, Nichole, Gigi, Davida, Maria, Gregory, Darlene, Marlon, and Imee. Many thanks to the friends and family who recently learned of the ministry and immediately offered their support and encouragement.

A special thanks to my family Teena, Cory and Holland who supported me at every step of the ministry. A special thanks to my wife Teena for your patience with my working all sorts of crazy hours for this ministry, especially during my 'stay-cation' of August 2023 to create this book. I am excited to be sharing this journey with you in life and all that the ministry is bringing into our lives. Thank you for the feedback and brainstorming and writing the back cover for the book.

Thank you to my mother, Maizie for your unwavering support. Thank you to my brothers Matthew, John, and Joseph who were enthusiastic supporters upon the announcement that I was launching this ministry on Thanksgiving Day of 2022.

Thank you to all of the staff and volunteers of Walking in Step With God Ministries. Your hard work and dedication are a blessing in so many ways and the ministry would not be where it is today without you. I look forward to the adventures ahead in 2024!

About This Book

This book is a collection of quotes from messages recorded at Walking In Step With God Ministries over the time period of August 2022 to August 2023.

Each 'chapter' of the book corresponds to a single message, 33 messages in all. For each message, there are up to 4 quotes extracted from a message.

In this SPECIAL EDITION of the book, for each quote, scripture is provided that offers context and/or foundation for the quote. Additionally, a prompt is provided for reflection about the quote

All Scripture quotations, unless otherwise indicated, are taken from the New King James Version Bible (NKJV).

All of the messages in this book can be found on the ministry website:

www.walkinginstepwithgod.org/messages

The messages contained in this book cover a range of topics. Messages can be viewed by topic on our website as well:

www.walkinginstepwithgod.org/topics

If the quotes in this book inspire and encourage you, I invite you to follow our ministry online to receive our regular content.

Find us on your favorite social media platform as "Walking in Step With God" or join our newsletter at:

www.walkinginstepwithgod.org/newsletter

If you prefer podcasts, you can find Walking in Step With God on Apple Podcasts, Spotify, or wherever you find your favorite podcasts.

When you purchase this book, you are granted an option to request a PDF version for printing or an alternate method of viewing.

To request a PDF version of the book, have your purchase receipt ready and visit:

www.walkinginstepwithgod.org/getbookpdf

May God use these quotes to lead you, guide you, and inspire you to strengthen your faith in Him. May He order your steps to His perfect plans for you.

Bless you.

Steve McDonald

About This Book

I can do all things through Christ who strengthens me.

- Philippians 4:13

How to Be a Light to the World

Help Those Who Are in Need

Is there a cause that is important to you?

Why not set aside some of your money to donate to the cause on a monthly basis?

Give, and it will be given to you: good measure, pressed down, shaken together, and running over will be put into your bosom. For with the same measure that you use, it will be measured back to you.

Luke 6:38

Do you donate on a regular basis to a cause important to you? Why do you donate?
_____
_____
_____
_____
_____
_____
_____
_____

One of the most wonderful things about walking with God is recognizing that often, your walk with Him can and will go beyond just you.

Give to him who asks you, and from him who wants to borrow from you do not turn away.

Matthew 5:42

Can you describe a recent time when you gave to someone in need? What did you give? How did your faith impact your giving?
_____
_____
_____
_____
_____
_____
_____

One of the most powerful ways we can help others in need is to ask God to use us to help others.

Sell what you have and give alms; provide yourselves money bags which do not grow old, a treasure in the heavens that does not fail,
where no thief approaches nor moth destroys.
For where your treasure is, there your heart will be also.

Luke 12:33-34

Can you recall a time when you recognized God used you to help someone in need? What was the need? How did you feel in the moment to respond to the need? Would you do it again?

_____
_____
_____
_____
_____
_____

How to Be a Light to the World

Do No Harm

Peace is a virtue that can be difficult to come by without a close and intimate walk with God.

Beloved, let us love one another, for love is of God; and everyone who loves is born of God and knows God.

1 John 4:7

Describe a time when you struggled to keep the peace and asked God for strength.

_____
_____
_____
_____
_____
_____
_____

God and only God can give us the strength to have love in our heart when harm has been inflicted upon us.

You shall not take vengeance, nor bear any grudge against the children of your people, but you shall love your neighbor as yourself: I am the LORD.

Leviticus 19:18

Have you ever taken revenge on someone who hurt you? If yes, explain why. If no, why not?
_____
_____
_____
_____
_____
_____
_____

In our walk with God, let us model how God is forgiving of us.

Seek a stance of forgiveness for those who have caused you harm.

And whenever you stand praying, if you have anything against anyone, forgive him, that your Father in heaven may also forgive you your trespasses.

Mark 11:25

When was the last time you forgave someone? Was it easy or difficult to forgive? In either case, explain why.

_____
_____
_____
_____
_____
_____
_____

How to Be a Light to the World

Honor Your Temple

How we deal with stress can affect how we show up for others.

In the multitude of my anxieties within me,
Your comforts delight my soul.

Psalm 94:19

Can you think of a time when stress, anxiety or worry kept you from assisting someone who was in need? How would you handle the situation the next time it occurs?

_____
_____
_____
_____
_____
_____

Ask God to give you guidance and discernment as to how to restructure your life in a way to be less overwhelmed.

*Therefore do not worry about tomorrow, for tomorrow
will worry about its own things.
Sufficient for the day is its own trouble.*

Matthew 6:34

Are you overwhelmed? If yes, will you ask God for assistance? If no, will you ask God to use you to help someone who is overwhelmed?

_____
_____
_____
_____
_____
_____
_____

In honoring your temple, you provide an environment for God to dwell in you and share His light through you to the world.

It is vain for you to rise up early,
To sit up late,
To eat the bread of sorrows;
For so He gives His beloved sleep.

Psalm 127:2

What is something you can do this week to cherish your temple?

_____
_____
_____
_____
_____
_____
_____

How to Be a Light to the World

Pray

While we may have a strong desire to be a light to the world, often there are areas of our life that we may need to address in order to properly be equipped to help others.

But you have not so learned Christ, if indeed you have heard Him and have been taught by Him, as the truth is in Jesus: that you put off, concerning your former conduct, the old man which grows corrupt according to the deceitful lusts, and be renewed in the spirit of your mind, and that you put on the new man which was created according to God, in true righteousness and holiness.

Ephesians 4:20-24

Is there an area of your life that you know needs work in order to be of service to others? What is the first step you can take to make progress on this work?

_____
_____
_____
_____
_____
_____

Ask God today and every day - not only for the opportunities to be a light to the world, but the courage and strength to act when the opportunity presents itself.

To be able to push through the hesitation and discomfort and maybe even fear.

To trust God is leading you and guiding you and equipping you to help that individual.

But do not forget to do good and to share, for with such sacrifices God is well pleased.

Hebrews 13:16

Can you think of a time that you hesitated to help someone in need? What will you do the next time you are in a position to help someone?

_____
_____
_____
_____
_____
_____
_____

Taking care of our whole self, mind, body and spirit creates a space in us for God's light to dwell and flourish.

Or do you not know that your body is the temple of the Holy Spirit who is in you, whom you have from God, and you are not your own?

1 Corinthians 6:19

What can you plan this year to take care of your mind, body and spirit? What can you plan for the years ahead to take better care of your whole self?

_____
_____
_____
_____
_____
_____
_____

How to Be a Light to the World

Acts of Kindness

The unexpected and even unwarranted gifts can be some of the most precious gifts of all.

And be kind to one another, tenderhearted, forgiving one another, even as God in Christ forgave you.

Ephesians 4:32

Can you describe a recent time when you performed a random act of kindness? How did it make you feel?

_____
_____
_____
_____
_____
_____
_____

Some of the most powerful forms of kindness are ones that are selfless.

Let each of you look out not only for his own interests, but also for the interests of others.

Philippians 2:4

Can you describe a time that someone performed a selfless act of kindness for you? How did it make you feel?

_____
_____
_____
_____
_____
_____
_____

Consider another approach to people who have wronged you.

Kindness.

Finally, all of you be of one mind, having compassion for one another; love as brothers, be tenderhearted, be courteous; not returning evil for evil or reviling for reviling, but on the contrary blessing, knowing that you were called to this, that you may inherit a blessing.

1 Peter 3:8-9

Can you describe a time someone wronged you and you did not retaliate? How did you practice kindness?

_____
_____
_____
_____
_____
_____

God in the Workplace

Ways to Walk With God at Work

In partnering with God, you can rest assured that your workplace experience is not limited to what you see and what you hear, but also the outcomes that God is orchestrating for you behind the scenes with your coworkers, including increase, protection, and favor.

Let Your work appear to Your servants,
And Your glory to their children.
And let the beauty of the LORD our God be upon us, And
establish the work of our hands for us;
Yes, establish the work of our hands.

Psalm 90:17

How do you partner with God at your place of work or school?

A boxer checks in with his coach between rounds, and a baseball player checks in with the coaches when they're in the dugout.

A football player checks in with the coaches during a timeout or when they're not on the field.

Why wouldn't we check in with God during our workday?

And take the helmet of salvation, and the sword of the Spirit, which is the word of God; praying always with all prayer and supplication in the Spirit, being watchful to this end with all perseverance and supplication for all the saints.

Ephesians 6:18

How does prayer help you in your workplace?

Whether you're in a corporate office, a small business, or a non-profit organization, integrating God into your work can transform your perspective and elevate your performance.

It helps you to view your work not just as a means to an end, but as an opportunity to serve others and glorify God.

Let your light so shine before men, that they may see your good works and glorify your Father in heaven.

Matthew 5:16

Can you provide an example of how your workplace is an opportunity to serve others and glorify God?
_____
_____
_____
_____
_____
_____
_____

God In The Workplace

Ways to Walk With God With Coworkers

One of the most powerful things we can do in our workplace is to align ourselves with God in our mannerisms, our words, and our actions.

Inevitably, as we align our hearts and minds with God, our coworkers will take notice as there is then an opportunity for them to see God's light shining through us, shining through you.

You are the light of the world. A city that is set on a hill cannot be hidden. Nor do they light a lamp and put it under a basket, but on a lampstand, and it gives light to all who are in the house. Let your light so shine before men, that they may see your good works and glorify your Father in heaven.

Matthew 5:14-16v

What traits about you are important to you to set an example for coworkers?
_____
_____
_____
_____
_____
_____
_____

In the workplace, disrupt the status quo and represent the light of God.

Do not allow yourself to go along with the way the world does things.

If you do this consistently, it will have a profound effect on others and even bring others closer to God.

Therefore be imitators of God as dear children. And walk in love, as Christ also has loved us and given Himself for us, an offering and a sacrifice to God for a sweet-smelling aroma.

Ephesians 5:1-2

If someone at work prompted you to 'go with the flow' and do an activity that did not honor God, what would you do?

_____
_____
_____
_____
_____
_____
_____

Being a light to coworkers is not just for those who seem to have it all together, but especially for those who are in need of kindness.

If you witness a coworker having a difficult time, express a word of kindness to them.

Remark to them that you hope they have a good day.

Provide a compliment or a word of encouragement.

Therefore, as the elect of God, holy and beloved, put on tender mercies, kindness, humility, meekness, longsuffering.

Colossians 3:12

Is there someone at your workplace that seems to be having a difficult time? How can you show kindness to them?

Is Your Reality Fair?

While we may not know what goes on behind closed doors with the faithful, God sees all.

If you are wondering why the friend you know who is faithful seems to have a level of blessing and anointing that is different from yours, consider that God may be waiting for a change in you.

Rest in the Lord, and wait patiently for Him; Do not fret because of him who prospers in his way, Because of the man who brings wicked schemes to pass.

Psalm 37:7

Do you know of someone who seems to have it all together, but scoffs at the idea of God? How can your walk with God benefit this individual?

You cannot partake in the comforts and norms of man and our culture, and still experience the same level of blessing and anointing that you would if you did not.

I say then: Walk in the Spirit, and you shall not fulfill the lust of the flesh. For the flesh lusts against the Spirit, and the Spirit against the flesh; and these are contrary to one another, so that you do not do the things that you wish.

Galatians 5:16-17

What are the habits or parts of your lifestyle that you know are not honoring God?

_____
_____
_____
_____
_____
_____
_____
_____

Many of us have heard of the term "The grass is not always greener on the other side."

This phrase rings true when it comes to observing others who are far from God and seem to have it all together as compared to the faithful when we are struggling.

Wait on the Lord,
And keep His way,
And He shall exalt you to inherit the land;
When the wicked are cut off, you shall see it.

Psalm 37:34

Is there someone in your life that you know is putting on a facade? How can you pray for them?
___
___
___
___
___
___
___
___

Don't Get Bitter

God knows what is best for you. Let us consider that while we may feel we know exactly what we need, God's will is always best.

Always.

The Lord is good to those who wait for Him,
To the soul who seeks Him.

Lamentations 3:25

Has there ever been a time in your life where you disagreed with God on what you need? Describe the what you felt you needed at the time and what God revealed to you.

_____
_____
_____
_____
_____

Have you considered that while you may feel you are ready for what you prayed for, God knows you are not?

Perhaps God has given you exactly what you seek, but orchestrated steps for you to be ready when the time is right.

For the Lord God is a sun and shield;
The Lord will give grace and glory;
No good thing will He withhold
From those who walk uprightly.

Psalm 84:11

Has there been a time in your life where you felt you were ready and God revealed that you were not? How did you proceed and why?

_____
_____
_____
_____
_____
_____
_____

When we are feeling angry at God, we must humbly bring ourselves before Him, the Creator of all things, and ask Him for direction. Remember, God loves you more than you can possibly wrap your head around.

God understands that we have emotions and can feel frustration when things are not clear.

The foolishness of a man twists his way,
And his heart frets against the Lord.

Proverbs 19:3

Have you ever been angry at God? Did you express your anger to Him or did you keep it bottled up? What did you learn from the experience?

_____
_____
_____
_____
_____
_____

Will He Say Yes, or No?

'No' may actually be 'Not now'.

There may be times that God in fact has said "Yes" to your petition but not at the timing you have in mind.

*To everything there is a season,
A time for every purpose under heaven.*

Ecclesiastes 3:1

Has God said 'No' to a prayer in your past but now you realize His answer at the time was actually 'Not now' or 'Not yet'? How did this experience affect your relationship with God and your faith overall?

_____
_____
_____
_____
_____

'No' may be to align us with God's will.

If we bring a prayer of petition before God that is not of His will, we should not expect Him to go against His own will.

Now this is the confidence that we have in Him, that if we ask anything according to His will, He hears us. And if we know that He hears us, whatever we ask, we know that we have the petitions that we have asked of Him.

1 John 5:14-15

Is there a time in your life when God said 'No' to a petition but you tried to make it happen anyway? What was the outcome?

_____
_____
_____
_____
_____
_____
_____

God is opening a door for you.

If we bring a prayer of petition before God, we may see His response [of 'Yes'] in the form of an opportunity that was not previously known.

For after all these things the Gentiles seek. For your heavenly Father knows that you need all these things. But seek first the kingdom of God and His righteousness, and all these things shall be added to you.

Matthew 6:32-33

Have you ever experienced an opportunity in your life that you feel was the result of God's influence? What was your reaction?

Celebrate in Your Trials

In our walk with God, He has never left our side. God is always with us—when times are good and when times are bad.

When we are experiencing trials in our lives, we must do our best to remember that God is with us and fully aware of every moment of our difficulty.

But may the God of all grace, who called us to His eternal glory by Christ Jesus, after you have suffered a while, perfect, establish, strengthen, and settle you.

1 Peter 5:10

Is there a time in your life where you struggled to believe that God was aware of your difficult circumstances? Describe why you felt this way.

_____
_____
_____
_____
_____
_____
_____

We must remember that, in our walk with God, we must not act as the world acts.

The world openly glorifies and encourages vengeance and retribution; however, as children of God we need not resort to such actions.

For one, vengeance for wrongdoing done to us belongs to God and God alone.

Beloved, do not avenge yourselves, but rather give place to wrath; for it is written, 'Vengeance is Mine, I will repay,' says the LORD.

Romans 12:19

Describe a time that you felt the desire to get revenge. Did you take things into your own hands or did you ask God for justice? In either case, explain your decision.

_____
_____
_____
_____
_____
_____

Let us also remember that times of trials and adversity may very well be part of a plan to draw us closer to God, strengthen our resolve, and equip us for a future where we learn to lean on God in every area of our lives.

My brethren, count it all joy when you fall into various trials, knowing that the testing of your faith produces patience. But let patience have its perfect work, that you may be perfect and complete, lacking nothing.

James 1:2-4

Has there been a time in your life where you experienced adversity but found refuge in God? Describe your experience.

_____
_____
_____
_____
_____
_____
_____

God Is Preparing You and Your Path

The most powerful thing we can do to have a full life is to walk with God and ask Him to lead and guide and prepare us according to His will.

*And I will wait on the LORD,
Who hides His face from the house of Jacob;
And I will hope in Him.*

Isaiah 8:17

Describe a time when you felt divinely led to go a different direction than you had originally planned.

God is the only one who can orchestrate events in your future to occur in such a way that is aligned perfectly with His perfect plan for you.

*For I know the thoughts that I think toward you, says the
LORD, thoughts of peace and not of evil, to give you a
future and a hope.*

Jeremiah 29:11

Has there been an experience in your life you are convinced was divinely ordered? Describe the experience and your reasoning that there was divine intervention.

_____
_____
_____
_____
_____
_____
_____

God will work with us at an intimate level to reveal the things that should be addressed in order for us to be prepared for His perfect plan for us.

*A prudent man foresees evil and hides himself;
The simple pass on and are punished.*

Proverbs 27:12

Has there been a change in your lifestyle or behavior that once existed but no longer does due to your walk of faith? Describe the change.

_____
_____
_____
_____
_____
_____
_____
_____

When It Seems All Is Lost

It is only human for us who walk in step with God to ask the question: 'Why God?'

It is only human for us to wonder why God may have allowed something to occur especially when we seek to align ourselves with God.

Be strong and of good courage, do not fear nor be afraid of them; for the LORD your God, He is the One who goes with you. He will not leave you nor forsake you.

Deuteronomy 31:6

Has there been a time in your life where your faith in God was tested due to difficult circumstances?
_____
_____
_____
_____
_____
_____
_____
_____

Ask God to give you strength for the things you don't even know will require strength.

Ask God to prop you up and keep you able to move forward, despite your emotions.

Our soul waits for the LORD;
He is our help and our shield.

Psalm 33:20

Has there been a time in your life when your strength was derived from your faith in God alone? Describe how your strength affected the circumstances at the time.

God may very well have shielded you from circumstances that are far worse than the circumstances you currently face.

As for God, His way is perfect;
The word of the LORD is proven;
He is a shield to all who trust in Him.

Psalm 18:30

Can you think of a time when you experienced adversity but know the circumstances could have been far worse? Provide an example or two of what could have occurred, but did not.

_____
_____
_____
_____
_____
_____

Who Do You Follow?

We can share information to uplift, encourage and inspire and we can share information to tear down, discredit and destroy.

A wholesome tongue is a tree of life,
But perverseness in it breaks the spirit.

Proverbs 15:4

Can you recall a time you spoke words that you regret were spoken? Describe the consequences of your words. Have you made an attempt to repair the damage done?

_____
_____
_____
_____
_____
_____

Do you look to gain wisdom from an individual who has millions of followers on social media or do you look to gain wisdom from God?

Remember the days of old,
Consider the years of many generations.
Ask your father, and he will show you;
Your elders, and they will tell you.

Deuteronomy 32:7

Can you think of an example of 'words of wisdom' that were imparted to you from someone older than you? What are the words? How have these words impacted your life?

_____
_____
_____
_____
_____
_____

Let us trust God's will in all of our plans and walk forward in faith with anticipation of His leading.

For You are my rock and my fortress;
Therefore, for Your name's sake,
Lead me and guide me.

Psalm 31:3

Can you describe a time when you knowingly walked forward in faith with expectation for God to direct you? What was the outcome?
_____
_____
_____
_____
_____
_____
_____

Keep Yourself Unspotted From the World

We all have opportunities to show the world how we display ourselves through our actions.

Bondservants, obey in all things your masters according to the flesh, not with eyeservice, as men-pleasers, but in sincerity of heart, fearing God. And whatever you do, do it heartily, as to the LORD and not to men.

Colossians 3:22-23

Can you recall something you recently did that is not typical of today's society, but honors God? What did you do? How did your faith influence your actions?

Let us lean on God to remain steadfast in a posture that prioritizes honoring God over honoring the status quo of what is popular in today's culture.

You shall diligently keep the commandments of the LORD your God, His testimonies, and His statutes which He has commanded you. And you shall do what is right and good in the sight of the LORD, that it may be well with you, and that you may go in and possess the good land of which the LORD swore to your fathers.

Deuteronomy 6:17-18

What is an example of a popular fact of today's culture that is considered the status quo but does not honor God?

Ask God for the strength and resolve to not bow to peer pressure when you are the only one who abstains from inappropriate behavior among close friends and family.

Ask God for courage when you need to enter an environment or a set of circumstances you know do not honor God, but your presence is needed.

Ask for the courage to remain firm in your posture of acting in an honorable way before God, even if there are strangers all around expecting you to go with the flow.

For the grace of God that brings salvation has appeared to all men, teaching us that, denying ungodliness and worldly lusts, we should live soberly, righteously, and godly in the present age.

Titus 2:12

Can you recall a time in a social setting where there were actions or activities that were not honoring God and you were put in a position to decline participation?

_____
_____
_____
_____
_____
_____

God Has Not Forgotten You

Only God knows the things that we do not know.

God knows what is happening behind the scenes in our circumstances and He knows what is best for us in every situation - even if what is best involves allowing us to experience unpleasant events in order to achieve a future outcome.

I know all the birds of the mountains,
And the wild beasts of the field are Mine.

Psalm 50:11

Can you think of a time that you had faith in God for a situation that was outside of your view? Describe the situation and the outcome.

_____
_____
_____
_____
_____
_____

As we have free will, we must choose to trust God with our circumstances and be cautious about trying to stay in control of every nuance of our circumstances.

I know all the birds of the mountains,
And the wild beasts of the field are Mine.

Psalm 50:11

Can you think of a time that you had faith in God for a situation that was outside of your view? Describe the situation and the outcome.

_____
_____
_____
_____
_____
_____
_____

As we have free will, we must choose to trust God with our circumstances and be cautious about trying to stay in control of every nuance of our circumstances.

The LORD is my strength and my shield;
My heart trusted in Him, and I am helped;
Therefore my heart greatly rejoices,
And with my song I will praise Him.

Psalm 28:7

Has there been a time in your life when you resisted giving up control to God? What did you seek to control at the time? Is there an area of your life today you seek to 'keep under your control' without God?

_____
_____
_____
_____
_____
_____

Pray that His will be done. This can be the most difficult step because we typically believe that we know everything about a difficult situation and that we know what the outcome should be.

The sooner we understand that God's will is the most important thing we should seek, the better off we will be.

Trust in the L<small>ORD</small> forever,
For in Y<small>AH</small>, the L<small>ORD</small>, is everlasting strength.

Isaiah 26:4

Has there been a recent event in your life where you yielded to God's will over your own will? Why did you yield to God's will?

_____
_____
_____
_____
_____
_____
_____
_____

Breaking Away From Bondage

Staying in the Word of God every day keeps our minds and hearts close to His instruction.

Be it a verse a day or a chapter a day, it is so important to keep our hearts and minds immersed in the Word.

All Scripture is given by inspiration of God, and is profitable for doctrine, for reproof, for correction, for instruction in righteousness, that the man of God may be complete, thoroughly equipped for every good work.

2 Timothy 3:16-17

Is there a Bible verse that inspires you and motivates you? What is the verse and how does it inspire you?

_____
_____
_____
_____
_____
_____
_____
_____

Human nature would have us feel as though when we fall into bondage from sinful behavior, that God could not possibly welcome us back

In fact, He is waiting for us with open arms.

If we confess our sins, He is faithful and just to forgive us our sins and to cleanse us from all unrighteousness.

1 John 1:9

Have you ever been in the middle of sinful behavior and stopped and turned to God in repentance in that moment? What was the behavior? Is the behavior still part of your life?

_____
_____
_____
_____
_____
_____
_____

We serve a loving and forgiving God, one who is there with us and ready to receive us when we turn away from our addiction and towards Him.

He who covers his sins will not prosper,
But whoever confesses and
forsakes them will have mercy.

Proverbs 28:13

What is a transgression you have kept to yourself and need to confess to God? Have you asked for forgiveness? If no, will you ask for forgiveness today?

_____
_____
_____
_____
_____
_____
_____

In the Face of Uncertainty

God is loving.

God is kind.

We can ask God for help, even if we are in the middle of a situation.

Keep in mind, each situation is different. However, God is always the same.

God is not going to love you less than if you had come to Him in the beginning.

He who dwells in the secret place of the Most High
Shall abide under the shadow of the Almighty.
I will say of the LORD,
'He is my refuge and my fortress;
My God, in Him I will trust'.

Psalm 91:1-2

Can you think of a time that you hesitated to turn to God because you were ashamed, embarrassed or prideful? What were the consequences of the hesitation?

_____
_____
_____
_____
_____
_____
_____

One of the most important things to do in the face of uncertainty is decide to partner with God.

*Eye has not seen, nor ear heard,
Nor have entered into the heart of man
The things which God has prepared for
those who love Him.*

1 Corinthians 2:9

Can you think of a time where you made a conscious decision to work with God with a situation in your life? What did you notice from God? What was the final outcome?

_____
_____
_____
_____
_____
_____
_____

God knows the appropriate way to help us when in need, even in the middle of chaos.

For God has not given us a spirit of fear, but of power and of love and of a sound mind.

2 Timothy 1:7

Can you describe a circumstance in your life where you were in the midst of chaos and you called out to God for help? What was the outcome?

_____
_____
_____
_____
_____
_____
_____

We can trust God when we are facing uncertainty. We can trust Him to provide what we need.

Perhaps we may not receive what we want, but most certainly - what we need.

The LORD will perfect that which concerns me;
Your mercy, O LORD, endures forever;
Do not forsake the works of Your hands.

Psalm 138:8

Can you describe a time in your life when God provided for your needs but it was different from what you thought you needed? How did you react in the moment? What was the outcome?

_____
_____
_____
_____
_____
_____
_____

Clay for the Potter

God can work with you as you are - be it flexible, be it rigid or be it broken into a million pieces.

Only God can mold and shape you and your life to receive His perfect vision for you - if you ask Him.

For we are His workmanship, created in Christ Jesus for good works, which God prepared beforehand that we should walk in them.

Ephesians 2:10

Do you feel broken or whole? Are you willing to be molded by God?

Something that is great about being a human being and God's child is that unlike the finished pottery from the kiln, we are moldable, flexible in how we behave, how we live our lives and how our actions can affect the lives of others.

But now, O LORD,
You are our Father;
We are the clay, and You our potter;
And all we are the work of Your hand.

Isaiah 64:8

How would you characterize yourself when it comes to being flexible and mold-able? In what ways do you consider yourself inflexible or rigid?

We all have the free will to say "I'm fine with things just as they are. I've got this."

We have the same free will to ask God to reveal to us what is keeping us from being aligned with His will for us...with His plans for us.

The humble He guides in justice,
And the humble He teaches His way.

Psalm 25:9

Can you recall a time that you felt you didn't need God? What was the outcome?

When God Wants Your Attention

Even if we are in a close and intimate walk with God, we are only human.

We can become flustered from events that are occurring in our day and we can even find ourselves overwhelmed with joy.

Let your eyes look straight ahead,
And your eyelids look right before you.
Ponder the path of your feet,
And let all your ways be established.
Do not turn to the right or the left;
Remove your foot from evil.

Proverbs 4:25-27

Have you ever been distracted from day to day life so much so that you turn your attention away from God? What did you notice?

_____
_____
_____
_____
_____
_____
_____

While He certainly does not have to - He loves us so very much that there are times He may intervene instead of simply allowing consequences of our actions that were lacking in good judgment.

I will deliver you from all your uncleannesses. I will call for the grain and multiply it, and bring no famine upon you.

Ezekiel 36:29

Can you recall an event in your life which you are certain you were saved by God despite your poor judgment at the time? Describe the event and the consequences that were averted.

_____
_____
_____
_____
_____
_____

You can experience signs from God, not just when you need help - but when He wants to lovingly and divinely tap you on the shoulder.

For I will not dare to speak of any of those things which Christ has not accomplished through me, in word and deed, to make the Gentiles obedient— in mighty signs and wonders, by the power of the Spirit of God, so that from Jerusalem and round about to Illyricum I have fully preached the gospel of Christ.

Romans 15:18-19

Have you experienced a sign from God? If so, describe the sign and how it impacted your faith from that moment forward.

_____
_____
_____
_____
_____
_____

Fighting Doubt

Talking to others in your life that you trust can provide you with comfort and assurance - no different than would be with other doubts in your life.

Counsel from someone you trust, including trusted members at your place of worship can be valuable in dismissing doubt.

*The way of a fool is right in his own eyes,
But he who heeds counsel is wise.*

Proverbs 12:15

Can you recall a time in your life that you sought wisdom from counsel? What was the advice you received? Did you act on the advice or ignore it?

God rewards those who are willing to have faith in Him.

He knows that it is our nature to be weary and suspect of holding trust in our hearts for things unseen and unknown.

Trust in the LORD with all your heart,
And lean not on your own understanding;

Proverbs 3:5

> Can you describe a time when you relied on your faith to navigate difficult circumstances? What were some of the emotions you felt at the time?

Trust God with your circumstances.

If you have thoughts of doubt, bring your concerns to God.

Find something in your life that you can bring to Him and decide to step forward in faith that He will reveal Himself to you.

Fear not, for I am with you;
Be not dismayed, for I am your God.
I will strengthen you, Yes, I will help you,
I will uphold you with My righteous right hand.

Isaiah 41:10

Is there an area of your life at this moment that you can walk forward in faith and trust God with the circumstances?

_____
_____
_____
_____
_____
_____

Why Should You Love Your Enemies?

God loves all of humanity, despite how humanity has mistreated and turned from Him over the ages.

God loves every human being on earth, regardless of their role in the world.

But God, who is rich in mercy, because of His great love with which He loved us, even when we were dead in trespasses, made us alive together with Christ (by grace you have been saved).

Ephesians 2:4-5

Is there someone in your life to whom you show love even though they have wronged you? How has your faith equipped you for this challenge?

_____
_____
_____
_____
_____
_____
_____

God asks us to show love to one another, regardless of who the individual may be - enemy or not.

But I say to you, love your enemies, bless those who curse you, do good to those who hate you, and pray for those who spitefully use you and persecute you.

Matthew 5:44

How do you show love to someone who has wronged you? Describe a recent situation where you showed love to someone that treated you with disrespect or rudeness.
_____
_____
_____
_____
_____
_____
_____

In praying for strength, guidance, and wisdom, we can show love to our enemies by practicing restraint and calm despite the individual's behavior.

Do not rejoice when your enemy falls,
And do not let your heart be glad when he stumbles;

Proverbs 24:17

How can God equip you today to not return evil for evil?

Divine Perfection in Imperfection

God is willing and able to give you strength, give you courage, give you the platform, give you the means, order your steps, open the doors, close the doors, and lay the path for you to accomplish His will despite what you feel are your imperfections.

Divine Perfection in Imperfection

God has chosen the foolish things of the world to put to shame the wise, and God has chosen the weak things of the world to put to shame the things which are mighty;

1 Corinthians 1:27

Do you feel there is an imperfection in you that is holding you back in your life? Do you believe that God can work through you despite this imperfection? If no, why?

_____
_____
_____
_____
_____
_____

Despite what your friends, family, co-workers or society labels you, you are perfectly made in the eyes of God.

Divine Perfection in Imperfection

For You formed my inward parts;
You covered me in my mother's womb.
I will praise You, for I am fearfully
and wonderfully made;
Marvelous are Your works,
And that my soul knows very well.

Psalm 139:13-14

What labels would society use to describe you? How would God describe you?

_____
_____
_____
_____
_____
_____
_____

God delights in doing extraordinary things with those of us who are ordinary, and even those of us whom society considers 'imperfect'.

But we have this treasure in earthen vessels, that the excellence of the power may be of God and not of us.

2 Corinthians 4:7

What gifts has God planted in you despite what society may label as 'imperfections'?

_____
_____
_____
_____
_____
_____
_____

Unanswered Prayer

Is It God or You?

Putting it very plainly and simply, we cannot expect to 'have our cake and eat it too' with God. Nor should we!

If you believe that God is the Creator and Master designer and King and holiest of holies and the Alpha and Omega then why would you expect Him to engage with someone who prioritizes Him over the world in the exact same way of someone that prioritizes the world over Him?

Therefore gird up the loins of your mind, be sober, and rest your hope fully upon the grace that is to be brought to you at the revelation of Jesus Christ; as obedient children, not conforming yourselves to the former lusts, as in your ignorance.

1 Peter 1:13-16

Is there an area of your life where you struggle turning away from the comforts of the world that do not honor God? Describe your most challenging struggle.

_____
_____
_____
_____
_____
_____

As we move away from the world, we may find ourselves ostracized and shunned, ridiculed and shamed for thinking we can move away from the creature comforts of man towards God.

You may be ridiculed when you stop using profanity among your friends, or attending your place of worship instead of hanging out.

You may experience an effect where your life starts to transform as you move towards God.

I wrote to you in my epistle not to keep company with sexually immoral people. Yet I certainly did not mean with the sexually immoral people of this world, or with the covetous, or extortioners, or idolaters, since then you would need to go out of the world.

1 Corinthians 5:9-10

Has your social life struggled as you moved away from norms of today's society and closer to God?

All of us are fallible and most importantly, we all sin.

*For there is not a just man on earth who does good
And does not sin.*

Ecclesiastes 7:20

How does the fact that we are all fallible affect your interactions with others? How does your faith affect your behavior around friends or co-workers who are comfortable with sin?

Trust in God's Plan, Not Your Own

He knows what you are made of.

He knows your strengths.

He knows your weaknesses.

He knows what you know about yourself, and He knows what you don't know about yourself.

God knows everything about you and every person you will ever meet for the rest of your life.

God knows your heart, and He knows your mind.

God knows a thing or two about you.

*You know my sitting down and my rising up;
You understand my thought afar off.*

Psalm 139:2

Is there something about you that you know God knows but you wish you knew? What will you ask God to reveal to you?

_____
_____
_____
_____
_____
_____
_____

While you may have the ability to create a plan for your future based on all the knowledge that you know, based on the education that you have pursued, based on advice and teaching, and guidance from others, only God knows a plan for your future that is perfected just for you.

*Commit your works to the LORD,
And your thoughts will be established.*

Proverbs 16:3

Do you share your plans with God in advance? What is the benefit of sharing your plans with God?

The most powerful thing we can do, even as we have free will and even as we have the ability to make our own choices, is to surrender our hearts and minds to God to follow His will for us.

Humble yourselves in the sight of the LORD,
and He will lift you up.

James 4:10

How do you feel when you surrender a situation to God? When is the last time you asked God to take over a difficult situation in your life? What was the outcome?

_____

_____

_____

_____

_____

_____

Vengeance Is Mine

If you are dealing with someone in your current day-to-day life that is treating you in an unjust way or doing things that are unfair to you, ask God for justice each day.

Ask God to defend you behind the scenes.

Ask God to orchestrate justice for you even if it is unbeknownst to you and out of your sight.

A false witness will not go unpunished,
And he who speaks lies will not escape.

Proverbs 19:5

Can you a describe a time in your life where you saw a change in circumstances when you asked God for justice? What was the change? Do you feel justice was served?

_____
_____
_____
_____
_____
_____
_____

It is absolutely and completely reasonable (and often necessary) to ask God each day - even each and every hour - as you are around this individual or individuals for the strength to not react in kind to the bad behavior being inflicted upon you.

Ask God to keep you safe.

Ask God to keep you strong.

Ask God to help you turn the other cheek.

Ask God for the will to not return evil for evil.

You have heard that it was said, 'An eye for an eye and a tooth for a tooth.' But I tell you not to resist an evil person. But whoever slaps you on your right cheek, turn the other to him also.

Matthew 5:38-39

Can you describe a time or situation in your life where you turned the other cheek? What was the situation? How, specifically, did you react or respond?
_____
_____
_____
_____
_____

When God says that vengeance is His, it means that He will handle it.

He will handle ensuring that justice is served to the individual or individuals who are persecuting you.

It means that He will repay the individual or individuals for the wrongs that have been done or are being done to you.

God will decide the appropriate response that is necessary for there to be justice.

*I will execute great vengeance on them with furious rebukes; and they shall know that I am the L*ORD*, when I lay My vengeance upon them.*

Ezekiel 25:17

Have you ever asked God for justice in a situation where you were wronged or harmed in some way? How did you cope as you awaited (or continue to await) justice?

_____
_____
_____
_____
_____
_____

Waiting on God

Waiting Out of Fear

The inner critic in us can be quite chatty when it comes to reminding us that we may fail or that something bad might happen.

So we may find ourselves -waiting- for a sign —before we try, —before we move, —before we walk forward trusting in God.

Be anxious for nothing, but in everything by prayer and supplication, with thanksgiving, let your requests be made known to God.

Philippians 4:6

How do you manage chatter and negative self-talk from your inner critic?

Will it feel warm and fuzzy when we move forward in faith?

Maybe not 100%, but knowing God is with us can in and of itself provide us with comfort that whatever happens, we have not been abandoned by our heavenly Father.

*Whenever I am afraid,
I will trust in You.
In God (I will praise His word),
In God I have put my trust;
I will not fear.
What can flesh do to me?*

Psalm 56:3-4

Is there an area of your life where you struggle to rely on your faith?
_____
_____
_____
_____
_____
_____
_____

God makes it very clear to us that we need not fear.

If we place our trust in Him, then we do not need a green light to walk forward.

We don't need a note or a text message before we act.

The LORD is on my side;
I will not fear.
What can man do to me?

- Psalm 118:6

Is there an area of your life in which fear is keeping you from moving forward? What fear can you bring before God today?

Waiting on God

Waiting on a Need

The word of God will guide us and instruct us in any and all things.

Let us turn to His word when in need when we are not sure what God has promised us or when we need reassurance that God has not left us or deserted us.

Especially when our circumstances can tempt us to think otherwise.

Wait on the LORD;
Be of good courage,
And He shall strengthen your heart;
Wait, I say, on the LORD!

Psalm 27:14

What Scripture do you turn to when you are waiting for God?

He knows that you did your best.

That you did it right.

That you honored Him in everything you do, yet still, you are in this situation.

He knows.

For the vision is yet for an appointed time;
But at the end it will speak, and it will not lie.
Though it tarries, wait for it;
Because it will surely come,
It will not tarry.

Habakkuk 2:3

Has there ever been a time in your life where you were waiting for God and felt that He did not fully realize the urgency of the situation? What was the outcome?

_____
_____
_____
_____
_____
_____

When we have brought something before God and we are waiting, know that you can lean into God while you wait.

You can lean into God, knowing and trusting that He knows your angst and worry and maybe even fear.

Having then gifts differing according to the grace that is given to us, let us use them: if prophecy, let us prophesy in proportion to our faith; or ministry, let us use it in our ministering; he who teaches, in teaching.

Romans 12:7

What does leaning into God look like for you?

Waiting on God

Making a Decision

God may even guide you with wisdom from counsel who do not believe in Him!

God may use others in your life who have "been there done that" and sprinkle wisdom from His Word to equip you in ways that you had not even considered.

Listen to counsel and receive instruction,
That you may be wise in your latter days.

Proverbs 19:20

Can you describe a time when you have provided counsel to someone in need? What were the circumstances in which you learned the advice you provided?
_____
_____
_____
_____
_____
_____

After you give your decision to God, move forward in what is reasonable, and have faith that He will correct you as you go. All this will direct you to an outcome that is aligned with His plan for you.

Through Your precepts I get understanding;
Therefore I hate every false way.

Psalm 119:104

Have you experienced a sign from God that steered you away from your original direction? What was the sign? What consequences were averted due to your change in direction?

_____
_____
_____
_____
_____
_____

If we keep our hearts and minds open to God's leading He will be faithful in providing signs for us to follow that will give us the guidance we need.

For example, opening and closing of doors or signs that appear as breadcrumbs on a path.

For a great and effective door has opened to me, and there are many adversaries.

1 Corinthians 16:9

Can you describe a time in your life when you know a door was closed due to God's intervention? How was your life changed or affected by God's intervention?

_____
_____
_____
_____
_____
_____

Freedom in Surrender

5 Ways You Can Experience Captivity When You Turn From God

When we don't seek God in the midst of our fears, anxiety and stress can run rampant.

We can become paralyzed.

God may have opened a door for us to grow and prosper, but we steer away from it out of fear and anxiety.

Therefore humble yourselves under the mighty hand of God, that He may exalt you in due time, casting all your care upon Him, for He cares for you.

2 Timothy 5:7

Can you describe a time in your life when you kept your fears to yourself instead of bringing your concern(s) to God? How did these fears affect your life?
_____
_____
_____
_____
_____
_____

Conflict cannot be completely avoided in our lives.

When we resist God we become more captive to our own reasoning and our emotions.

Without God, peace in our heart and mind escapes us.

Without peace, strife and explosive conflict can become inevitable when faced with challenges and confrontations with others.

Let all bitterness, wrath, anger, clamor, and evil speaking be put away from you, with all malice.

Ephesians 4:31

What do you do to maintain peace in your heart?

When we resist turning to God for healing and for comfort, we may find ourselves suffering more intensely and longer than needed.

Heal me, O LORD, and I shall be healed;
Save me, and I shall be saved,
For You are my praise.

Jeremiah 17:14

Have you or someone you know experienced healing as the result of prayer?

Freedom in Surrender

5 Ways You Can Experience Freedom When You Turn to God

When we surrender ourselves to God, what we can know is that His word says we need not live in fear.

The LORD is my light and my salvation;
Whom shall I fear?
The LORD is the strength of my life;
Of whom shall I be afraid?

Psalm 27:1

Can you describe a time in your life when your fears were subdued due to your trust in God? How do you manage fear in your life today?

_____
_____
_____
_____
_____
_____
_____
_____

Surrendering your life to God, and surrendering your struggle with addiction to God He can facilitate a path for you to move you towards recovery and a better life for yourself.

No temptation has overtaken you except such as is common to man; but God is faithful, who will not allow you to be tempted beyond what you are able, but with the temptation will also make the way of escape, that you may be able to bear it.

1 Corinthians 10:13

Is there a time in your life when you struggled with addiction? How has your faith contributed to your journey through recovery?

When we surrender our heart to God, He can intervene and orchestrate things in such a way to make sure that we always have what we need.

We may not have what we want, but in surrendering to God, He promises to provide what we need.

And my God shall supply all your need according to His riches in glory by Christ Jesus.

Philippians 4:19

Can you recall a time when God provided you with precisely what you needed? What did you feel you needed? What did God provide?

_____
_____
_____
_____
_____
_____
_____

How to Give Your Heart Fully to God

Envy, lust, greed, and vengeance are just a few of the norms that society feels are acceptable, but, in fact, are sins before God.

We can give our hearts fully to God by taking a posture that turns away from the norms of the world to honor God in all of our ways.

And do not be conformed to this world, but be transformed by the renewing of your mind, that you may prove what is that good and acceptable and perfect will of God.

Romans 12:2

What is a habit or behavior in your life that you would like to do more of or less of to please God?

_____
_____
_____
_____
_____
_____
_____
_____

Only God can guide us to a plan that He knows will transform us from the inside out.

Only God can show us a plan that provides everlasting peace and joy that defies understanding.

Be anxious for nothing, but in everything by prayer and supplication, with thanksgiving, let your requests be made known to God; and the peace of God, which surpasses all understanding, will guard your hearts and minds through Christ Jesus.

Philippians 4:7

Have you asked God to reveal His plan for you? If yes, what was the outcome? If no, why not?

_____
_____
_____
_____
_____
_____
_____

God has created each and every one of us and He knows what is best for us.

When we can find it in our heart to serve Him and trust Him, even if His plan is not quite what we had in mind, we can find a level of fulfillment and contentment that can only come from serving Him and walking in step with Him each and every day.

The Lord also will be a refuge for the oppressed,
A refuge in times of trouble.
And those who know Your name will put their trust in
You; For You, Lord, have not forsaken those who seek You.

Psalm 9:9-10

Have you ever received a sign from God to proceed with a plan that you did not expect? Describe the sign and how you responded.

_____
_____
_____
_____
_____
_____
_____

God Is in the Room

We can ask God to touch our hearts and help us to know His presence is near.

We can ask God for peace and peace of mind in our circumstances.

We can ask Him to fill the gaps of loneliness with His love and His light.

Where can I go from Your Spirit?
Or where can I flee from Your presence?

Psalm 139:7

Have you experienced a time when you felt God's presence was near? How did it feel? Describe your emotions in that moment.

_____
_____
_____
_____
_____
_____
_____

Make no mistake, God is in the room.

He is in the room with you right now.

We can truly have a transformative life if we walk through our day, knowing this truth.

Knowing that wherever we go, God is with us.

Have I not commanded you? Be strong and of good courage; do not be afraid, nor be dismayed, for the L<small>ORD</small> your God is with you wherever you go.

Joshua 1:9

Have you experienced a moment in your life when you believe God intervened in circumstances that were unfolding in real time? Describe the moment(s) of intervention.
_____
_____
_____
_____
_____
_____
_____

We may experience pain and suffering even as God is in the room but know that God can make good out of the evil deeds done to you. Know that God can see to it there is justice.

Trust God and seek out God in all you do.

If suffering does come upon you, ask Him to lead and guide your circumstances according to His perfect plan and outcome.

For I, the LORD *your God, will hold your right hand, Saying to you, 'Fear not, I will help you'.*

Isaiah 41:13

Have you ever asked God for justice on your behalf? What was the injustice? What was the eventual outcome?

_____
_____
_____
_____
_____
_____
_____

Closing Prayer

Father God,

Thank You for the words of wisdom and direction offered in this book.

We pray that You will continue to teach, guide, and order our steps as we walk with You each day.

Help us to know of Your presence - both in times of peace and in times of adversity - In times of abundance and times of lack. Help us to know You are near regardless of how things may appear in the natural.

Remind us of the words of wisdom offered in this book when our thoughts and our actions lead us astray. Give us the signs to keep us aligned with the perfect plans you have in store for us.

May Your light shine brightly in our lives and in our hearts as we strive each day to walk in step with You.

- Amen

Notes

We hope the preceding pages have inspired you to trust God with every fiber of your being! If you would like to access any of the full-length messages in this book, please visit:

www.walkinginstepwithgod.org/messages

There, you will find the video and transcript for each message, along with a 'Going Deeper With the Word' segment where we dive into God's Word following each message. You can also find Walking In Step With God messages videos on YouTube:

www.youtube.com/@walkinginstepwithgod

If you prefer podcasts, you can find Walking in Step With God on Apple Podcasts, Spotify, or wherever you find your favorite podcasts.

If you enjoyed reading this book, we would be grateful if you could leave a review on the retailer's site you purchased the book or on Goodreads.

Bless you!

Made in the USA
Middletown, DE
21 October 2024